Mary
and the Angel

Bibleworld Books contains stories adapted
from the *Contemporary English Version* of the Bible.
Each book is designed to provide early readers with a text
adapted from Scripture in a form and manner that helps them
develop their reading skills and introduce them to the narrative of the Bible.

Adapted from:
Mission Literacy Readers Level 1 & 2
© 2008 American Bible Society
Used by permission.

Mary and the Angel is based on Luke 1:26-49

ISBN 978-0-901518-84-2

Series 4: Book 1

Illustrated by Graeme Hewitson

SCOTTISH
BIBLE SOCIETY
The Word for the world

The Scottish Bible Society
7 Hampton Terrace, Edinburgh. EH12 5XU
www.scottishbiblesociety.org

BIBLEWORLD BOOKS

Series 4: The Story of Jesus' Birth

Mary and the Angel
Jesus is Born

**Bibleworld Books provides three full session outlines
to accompany each story book with games and activities
designed to raise each child's learning potential.**

Available for free download at www.bibleworld.co.uk

Mary was a young girl who lived in the town of Nazareth

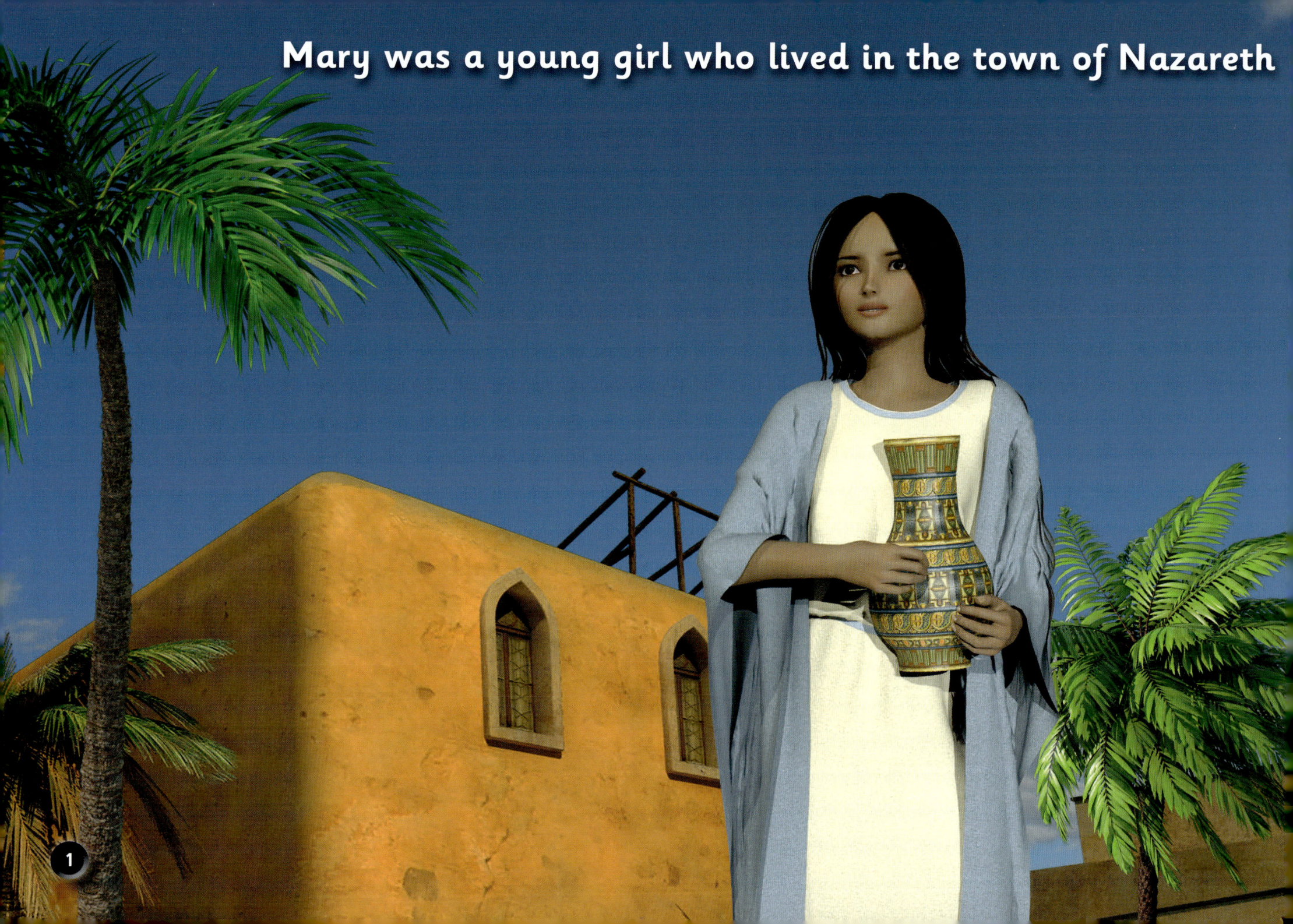

and was engaged to a man named Joseph.

One day God sent the angel Gabriel to her with a message.

"Hello, Mary!" the angel said.
"You are truly blessed!"

Mary was puzzled.
What could those words mean?

"Don't be afraid," the angel said.

"God is pleased with you, Mary.

You will have a son,
and his name will be Jesus."

"But how could such a thing happen, since I'm not married?" Mary asked.

"Nothing is impossible for God," the angel told her.

"God's power will do this...

and your son will be called the Son of God."

10

"All right," Mary said. "I will do what God wants me to do." And the angel left.

Soon afterward, Mary went to visit Elizabeth, who was going to have a baby too.

Mary walked from Nazareth to Elizabeth's house in the hills. Upon her arrival, she went inside, calling out to Elizabeth.

Elizabeth answered, "Mary, God has blessed you and your child!"

14

"When you spoke, my baby leaped for joy inside me!"

Mary was so happy that
she sang a song;
here is part of it.

"With all my heart I praise the Lord, and I rejoice in God my Saviour."